PIANO • VOCAL • GUITAR

2nd Edition

Great American
COUNTRY
songbook

ISBN 978-0-8818-8745-7

HAL•LEONARD®
CORPORATION
7777 W. BLUEMOUND RD. P.O. BOX 13819 MILWAUKEE, WI 53213

Visit Hal Leonard Online at
www.halleonard.com

CONTENTS

ALL I HAVE TO DO IS DREAM

Words and Music by
BOUDLEAUX BRYANT

ALL THE GOLD IN CALIFORNIA

Words and Music by
LARRY GATLIN

for - nia, _____ it don't mat - ter at all _____ where you've played _____

_____ be - fore; _____ Cal - i - for - nia's a brand - new _____ game. _____

Try - in' to be a he - ro, _____ wind - ing up a ze - ro, _____

can scar a man for - ev - er _____ right down to your soul. _____

ANY DAY NOW

Words and Music by BOB HILLIARD
and BURT BACHARACH

BACK IN THE SADDLE AGAIN

Words and Music by GENE AUTRY
and RAY WHITLEY

back in the sad - dle a - gain.

Rid - in' the range once more,

tot - in' my old for - ty - four; where you

sleep out ev - 'ry night, where the on - ly law is right, I'm

ANY TIME

Words and Music by
HERBERT HAPPY LAWSON

BLUE MOON OF KENTUCKY

Words and Music by
BILL MONROE

Bright Jump tempo

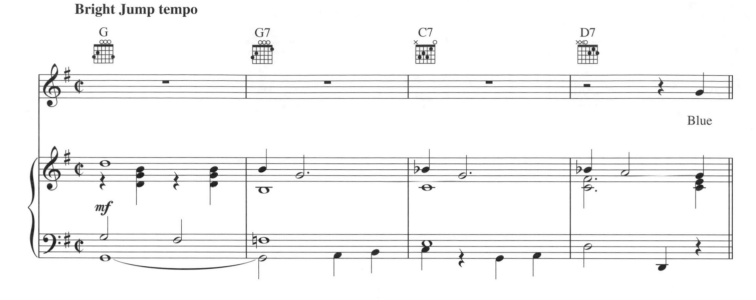

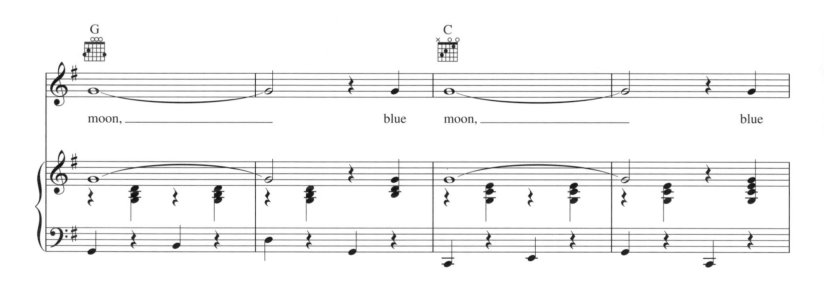

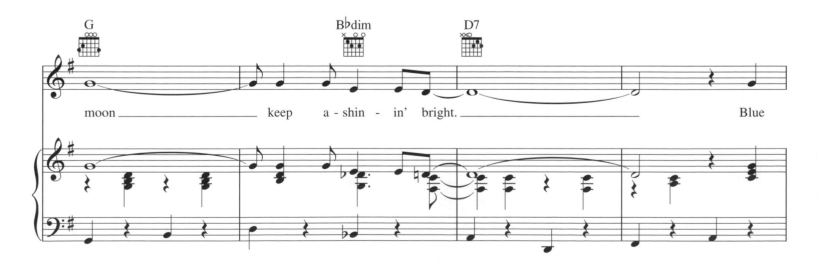

BONAPARTE'S RETREAT

Words and Music by REDD STEWART
and PEE WEE KING

BORN TO LOSE

Words and Music by
TED DAFFAN

BOOT SCOOTIN' BOOGIE

Words and Music by
RONNIE DUNN

heel to toe, do - cie doe, come on, ba - by, let's go

boot scoot-in'!   Whoa, __   Cad - il - lac,   Black - jack,

ba - by meet me out back, we're gon - na boo - gie.

Oh, __   get down   turn a - round, __   go to town, __   boot scoot-in'

BUTTERFLY KISSES

Words and Music by BOB CARLISLE
and RANDY THOMAS

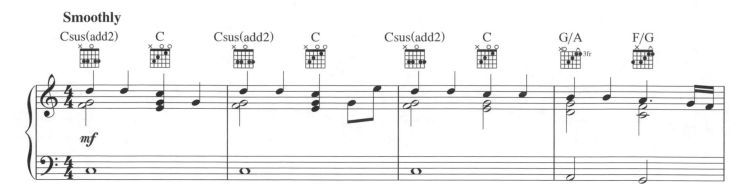

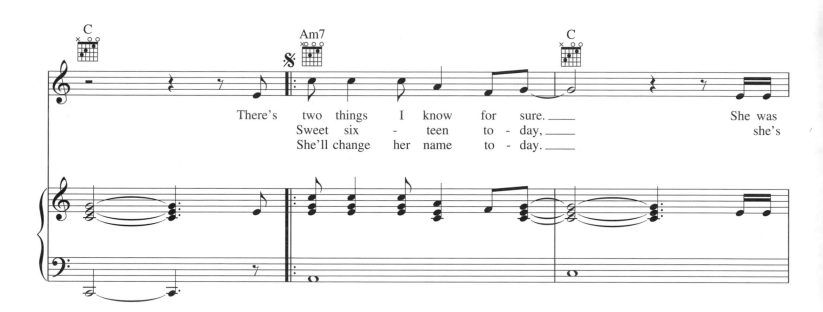

There's two things I know for sure. _____ She was
Sweet six - teen to - day, _____ she's
She'll change her name to - day. _____

sent here from heav - en, and she's dad - dy's lit - tle girl. _____ As I
look - ing like her mom - ma a lit - tle more ev - 'ry day. _____
She'll make a prom - ise, and I'll give her a - way.

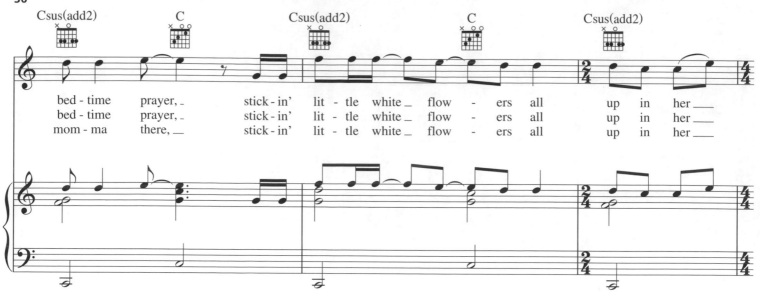

bed - time prayer, _____ stick - in' lit - tle white _ flow - ers all up in her ___
bed - time prayer, _____ stick - in' lit - tle white _ flow - ers all up in her ___
mom - ma there, ___ stick - in' lit - tle white _ flow - ers all up in her ___

hair. "Walk be - side ___ the po - ny, Dad - dy, it's
hair. "You know how much ___ I love ___ you, Dad - dy, but if
hair. "Walk me down ___ the aisle, ___ Dad - dy, it's

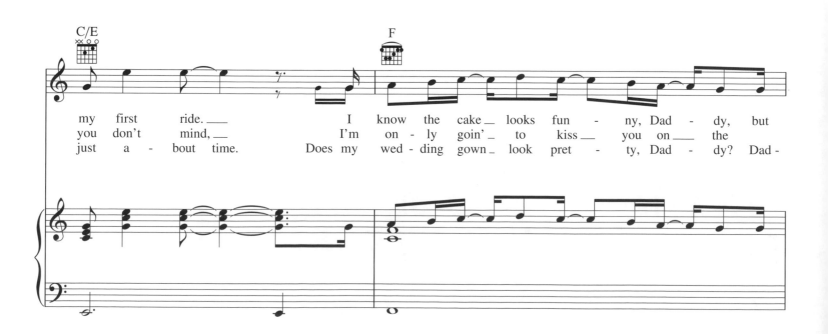

my first ride. ___ I know the cake ___ looks fun - ny, Dad - dy, but
you don't mind, ___ I'm on - ly goin' ___ to kiss ___ you on ___ the
just a - bout time. Does my wed - ding gown _ look pret - ty, Dad - dy? Dad -

CAN THE CIRCLE BE UNBROKEN
(Will the Circle Be Unbroken)

Words and Music by
A.P. CARTER

THE CLOSER YOU GET

Words and Music by JAMES PENNINGTON
and MARK GRAY

The clos - er you get, _____

CHATTAHOOCHEE

Words and Music by JIM McBRIDE
and ALAN JACKSON

Bright Country 2-step

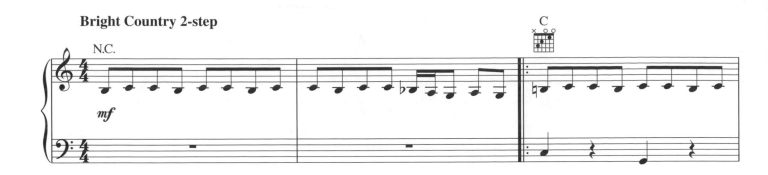

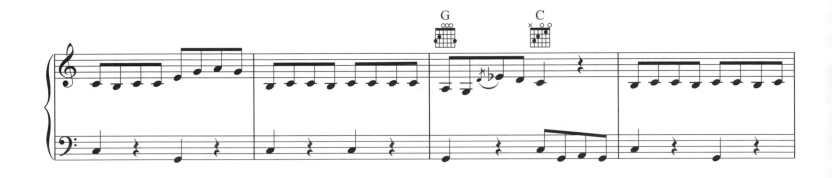

Way down yon - der on the Chat - ta - hoo - chee

Well, we fogged up the win - dows in ___ my old Chev - y;

it gets hot - ter than a hoo - chie coo - chie. We laid rub - ber on the
I was will - in' but __ she was - n't read - y. So, I set - tled for a bur - ger and a

Geor - gia as - phalt. Got a lit - tle cra - zy but we nev - er got caught.
grape sno - cone. __ I dropped her off __ ear - ly but I did - n't go home.

(1., 2.) Down by the riv - er on a Fri - day night, __ pyr - a - mid of cans in the
(D.S.) *Instrumental solo*

pale moon - light, talk - ing 'bout cars and dream - in' 'bout wom - en.

COLD, COLD HEART

Words and Music by
HANK WILLIAMS

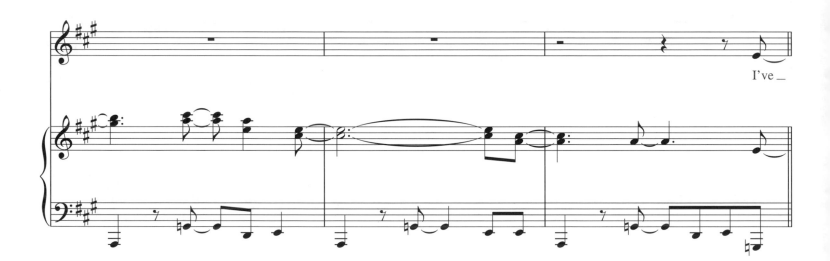

I've

tried so hard, my dear, _____ to show _____ that you're my _ ev - 'ry dream, _

for things I ___ did-n't ___ do. ___ In ___ an - ger, un - kind

words I said ___ that make the tear-drops start. _____ Why can't ___

___ I free ___ your doubt - ful mind ___ and melt your cold, ___ cold, ___

___ heart? ___

There was a time when I be-lieved _ that you be-longed _ to me, _ but now I know your heart is shack-led to a ___ mem - o - ry. ___ The more I learn to

care for you, ___ the more we drift a-part. _____ Why

can't I free _____ your doubt-ful mind _____ and melt _ your cold, _ cold _____

_____ heart? _____

COWARD OF THE COUNTY

Words and Music by ROGER BOWLING
and BILLY EDD WHEELER

Ev-'ry-one __ con-sid-ered him __ the cow-ard of __ the coun - ty. __

He'd nev-er stood __ one sin-gle time to prove the coun-ty wrong. __

__ His ma-ma named __ him Tom-my, the

folks just called him yel - low. _ But some-thing al - ways

told me they were read - in' Tom - my wrong. _

He was on - ly ten _ years old _ when his dad - dy died _ in pris - on. _

I looked af - ter Tom - my 'cause he was my broth - er's son. _

some - one for ev - 'ry - one __ and Tom-my's love __ was Beck-y. __

In her arms __ he did-n't have __ to prove he was a man. __

One day while he was work - in' _____ the

Gat-lin boys __ came call - in'. They took turns __ at Beck-

(Spoken:) There was three of them!

Tom-my o - pened up ___ the door ___ and saw his Beck - y cry - in'.

The torn dress, the shat-tered look ___ was more than he ___ could

stand.

He reached a - bove ___ the fire - place and took

CRYIN' TIME

Words and Music by
BUCK OWENS

Now they say that ab-sence makes the heart grow fond-er, _____ and that tears are on-ly rain to make love

grow. Well, my love for you could nev-er grow no strong-er, _____ if I

lived to be a hun - dred years old. Oh, it's

cry - in' time a - gain, you're gon - na leave me, ____ I can

see that far - a - way look ____ in your eyes. I can

tell ____ by the way you ____ hold me, dar - lin', that it

DADDY SANG BASS

Words and Music by
CARL PERKINS

DADDY DON'T YOU WALK SO FAST

Words and Music by PETER CALLENDER
and GEOFF STEPHENS

DEEP IN THE HEART OF TEXAS

Words by JUNE HERSHEY
Music by DON SWANDER

DETROIT CITY

Words and Music by DANNY DILL
and MEL TILLIS

Hard-driving Country

Last night I went to sleep in De - troit Cit - y,
Home folks think I'm big in De - troit Cit - y.

and I dreamed a - bout the cot - ton fields and home.
From the let - ters that I write, they think I'm fine.

I
But by

DOWN AT THE TWIST AND SHOUT

Words and Music by
MARY CHAPIN CARPENTER

Fast Country Two-Beat

Sat-ur-day night and the moon is out.__ I wan-na head on o-ver to the Twist and Shout, find a two-step part-ner and a Ca-jun beat. When it lifts me up,__ I'm gon-na

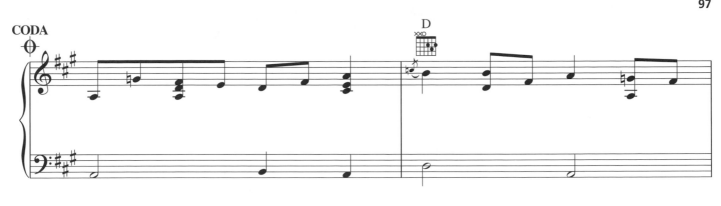
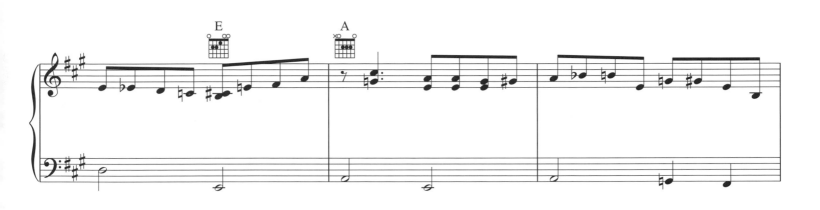

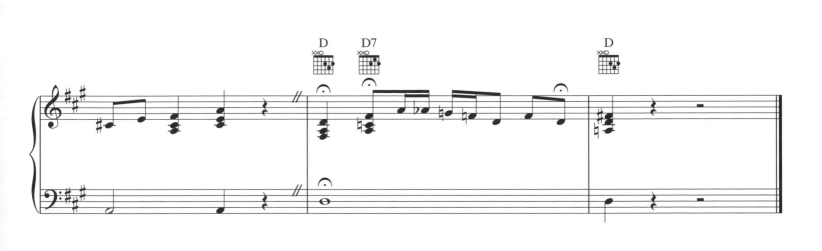

THE GAMBLER

Words and Music by
DON SCHLITZ

DREAM BABY
(How Long Must I Dream)

Words and Music by
CINDY WALKER

EL PASO

Words and Music by
MARTY ROBBINS

girl.

whirl.

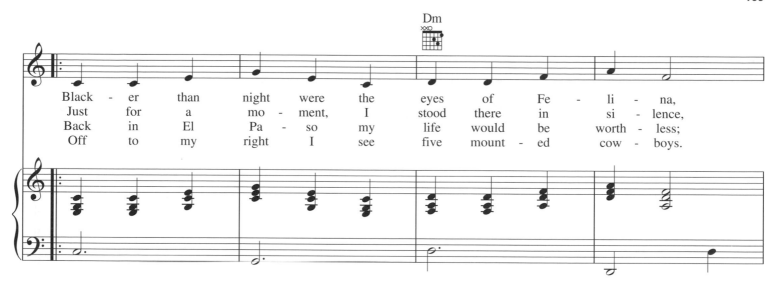

Black - er than night were the eyes of Fe - li - na,
Just for a mo - ment, I stood there in si - lence,
Back in El Pa - so my life would be worth - less;
Off to my right I see five mount - ed cow - boys.

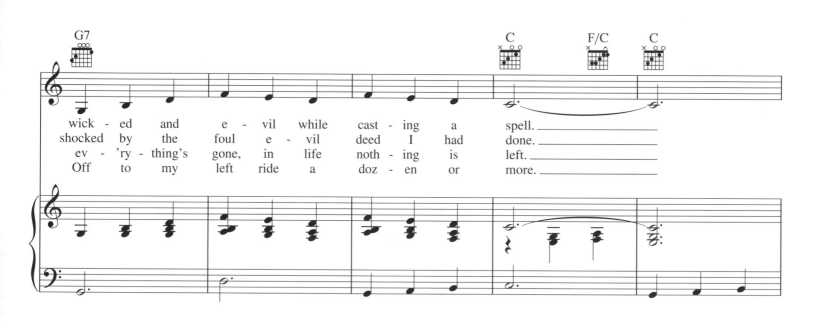

wick - ed and e - vil while cast - ing a spell.
shocked by the foul e - vil deed I had done.
ev - 'ry - thing's gone, in life noth - ing is left.
Off to my left ride a doz - en or more.

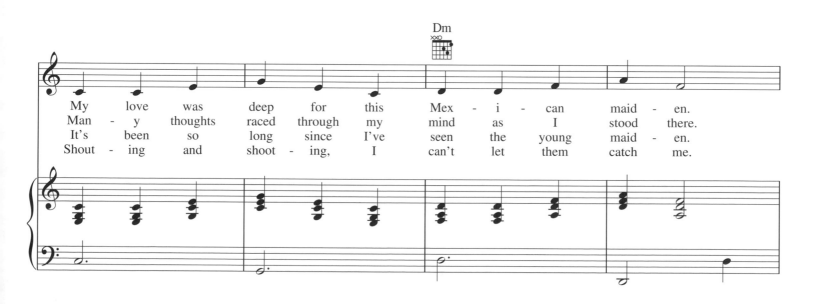

My love was deep for this Mex - i - can maid - en.
Man - y thoughts raced through my mind as I stood there.
It's been so long since I've seen the young maid - en.
Shout - ing and shoot - ing, I can't let them catch me.

I was in love, but in vain, I could tell._____
I had but one chance, and that was to run._____
My love is strong-er than my fear of death._____
I have to make it to Ro-sa's back door._____

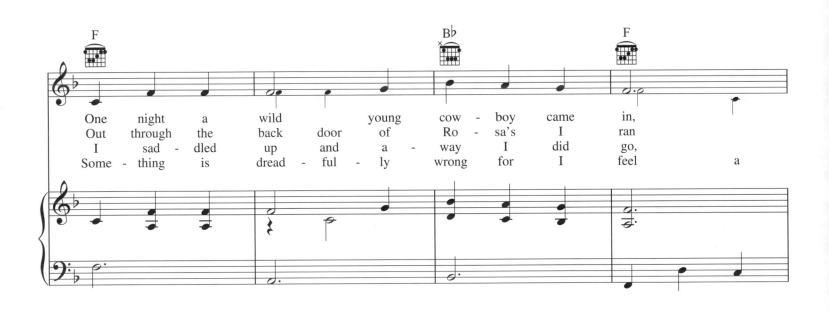

One night a wild young cow-boy came in,
Out through the wild back door of Ro-sa's I ran
I sad-dled up and a-way I did go,
Some-thing is dread-ful-ly wrong for I feel a

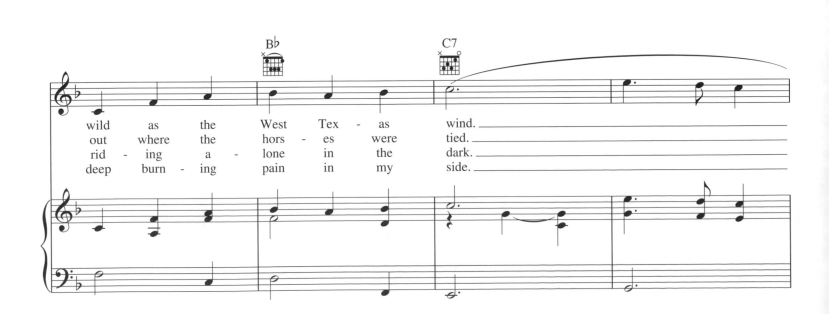

wild as the West Tex-as wind._____
out where the hors-es were tied._____
rid-ing a-lone in the dark._____
deep burn-ing pain in my side._____

Dash - ing and dar - ing, a
I caught a good one, it
May - be to - mor - row a
Though I am try - ing to

drink he was shar - ing with wick - ed Fe - li - na, the
looked like it could run. _____ Up - on its back and a -
bul - let will find me. To - night, noth - ing's worse than this
stay in the sad - dle, _____ I'm get - ting wea - ry, un -

girl that I loved. _____ So, in an - ger, I
way I did ride _____ just as fast as I
pain in my heart. _____ And at last, here I
a - ble to ride. _____ But my love for Fe -

chal - lenged his right for the love of this maid - en.
could from the right West Tex - as town of El Pa - so,
am on the hill o - ver - look - ing El Pa - so,
li - na is strong and I rise where I've fall - en.

Down went his hand for the gun that he wore. _____
out to the bad - lands of New Mex - i - co. _____
I can see Ro - sa's Can - ti - na be - low. _____
Though I am wea - ry, I can't stop to rest. _____

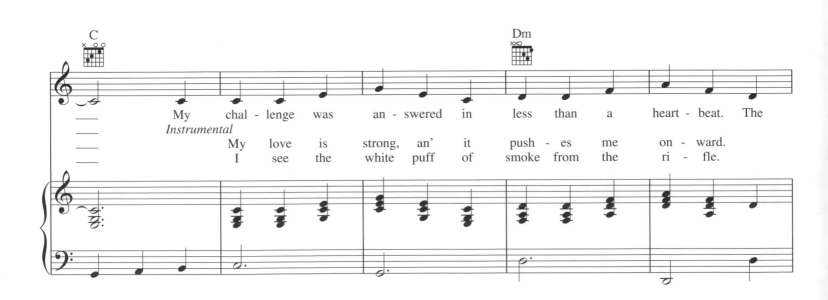

_____ My chal - lenge was an - swered in less than a heart - beat. The
_____ *Instrumental*
_____ My love is strong, an' it push - es me on - ward.
_____ I see the white puff of smoke from the ri - fle.

Play 4 times

hand - some young stran - ger lay dead on the floor. _____
Instrumental ends
Down off the hill to Fe - li - na I go. _____
I feel the bul - let go deep in my chest. _____

From out of no - where, Fe - li - na has found me,
Cra - dled by two lov - ing arms that I'll die for,

kiss - ing my cheek as she kneels by my side. _____
one lit - tle kiss, then, Fe - li - na, good -

bye. _____

FAMILY TRADITION

Words and Music by
HANK WILLIAMS, JR.

1. Coun - try mu - sic sing - ers have al - ways been a real close fam - i -
2., 3. *(See additional lyrics)*

ly,   but late - ly some of my kin - folk have dis -

owned a few oth - ers and me. _____   I guess it's be -

Additional Lyrics

2. I am very proud of my daddy's name,
   Although his kind of music and mine ain't exactly the same.
   Stop and think it over, put yourself in my position.
   If I get stoned and sing all night long, it's a family tradition.

   So don't ask me, "Hank,
   Why do you drink?
   Hank, why do you roll smoke?
   Why must you live out the songs that you wrote?"
   If I'm down in a honky-tonk, some old slicks tryin' to give me friction
   I say leave me alone, I'm singin' all night long, it's a family tradition.

3. Lordy, I have loved some ladies and I have loved Jim Beam,
   And they both tried to kill me in nineteen seventy-three.
   When that doctor asked me, "Son, how'd you get in this condition?"
   I said, "Hey, sawbones, I'm just carryin' on an old family tradition."

   So don't ask me, "Hank,
   Why do you drink?
   Hank, why do you roll smoke?
   Why must you live out the songs that you wrote?"
   Stop and think it over, try to put yourself in my unique position.
   If I get stoned and sing all night long, it's a family tradition.

FOLSOM PRISON BLUES

Words and Music by
JOHN R. CASH

1. I hear the train a - com - in'. it's roll - in' 'round the
2. I was just a ba - by my ma - ma told me,
3.,4. *(See additional lyrics)*

bend, And I ain't seen the sun - shine since I don't know
"Son, al - ways be a good boy; don't ev - er play with

when. I'm stuck at Fol - som Pris - on and time keeps
guns." But I shot a man in Re - no just to

Additional Lyrics

3. I bet there's rich folks eatin' in a fancy dining car;
   They're prob'ly drinkin' coffee and smokin' big cigars.
   But I know I had it comin', I know I can't be free,
   But those people keep a-movin', and that's what tortures me.

4. Well, if they freed me from this prison, if that railroad train was mine,
   I bet I'd move on over a little farther down the line.
   Far from Folsom Prison, that's where I want to stay,
   And I'd let that lonesome whistle blow my blues away.

GENTLE ON MY MIND

Words and Music by
JOHN HARTFORD

riv - ers of my mem-'ry that keeps you ev - er gen - tle on my

mind.

It's

mind.

Additional Lyrics

2. It's not clinging to the rocks and ivy planted on their columns now that binds me,
   Or something that somebody said because they thought we fit together walkin'.
   It's just knowing that the world will not be cursing or forgiving when I walk along
   Some railroad track and find
   That you're moving on the backroads by the rivers of my memory, and for hours
   You're just gentle on my mind.

3. Though the wheat fields and the clotheslines and junkyards and the highways
   Come between us,
   And some other woman crying to her mother 'cause she turned and I was gone.
   I still run in silence, tears of joy might stain my face and summer sun might
   Burn me 'til I'm blind,
   But not to where I cannot see you walkin' on the backroads by the rivers flowing
   Gentle on my mind.

4. I dip my cup of soup back from the gurglin' cracklin' caldron in some train yard,
   My beard a roughening coal pile and a dirty hat pulled low across my face.
   Through cupped hands 'round a tin can I pretend I hold you to my breast and find
   That you're waving from the backroads by the rivers of my memory, ever smilin',
   Ever gentle on my mind.

GOD BLESS THE U.S.A.

Words and Music by
LEE GREENWOOD

Am7　Gm7

liv - in' here __ to - day, __ 'cause the flag still stands for free - dom and they

Dm　B♭

can't take that a - way. _____ And I'm

C/E　B♭/D　F

proud to be an A - mer - i - can __ where at least I know I'm free. And I

C/E　B♭/D　F

won't for - get the men who died, who gave that right to me. And I'd glad - ly

HALF AS MUCH

Words and Music by
CURLEY WILLIAMS

HAPPY TRAILS

from the Television Series THE ROY ROGERS SHOW

Words and Music by
DALE EVANS

E♭7
A♭maj7
A♭6
3fr
cares a - bout the clouds when we're to - geth - er? Just
C7
F9
B♭7
sing a song and bring the sun - ny weath - er. Hap - py
E♭
3fr
B♭m6
6fr
C7
Fm
B♭7
trails to you till we meet a -
1
E♭
3fr
B♭7
gain. Hap - py
2
E♭
3fr
A♭
4fr
E♭6
gain.

HUSBANDS AND WIVES

Words and Music by
ROGER MILLER

Two bro-ken hearts, lone-ly, look-in' like hous-es where no-bod-y lives.

Two peo-ple each hav-in' so much pride in-side, nei-ther side for-

To Coda ⊕

de - cline in the num - ber _____ of hus - bands and

wives.

A wom - an and a man, a man and a wom - an,

some can, some can't, and some __ can't. _____

num - ber _____ of hus - bands and wives.

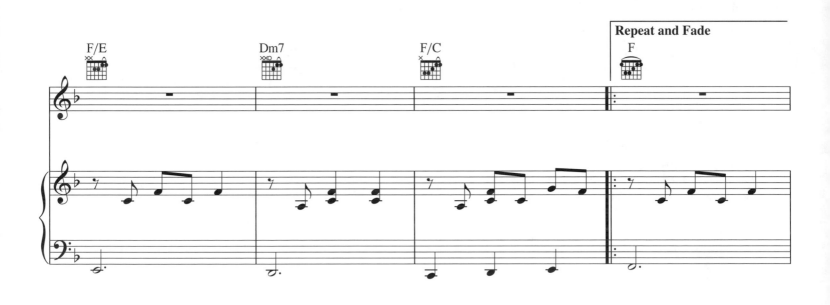

Repeat and Fade

I WOULDN'T HAVE MISSED IT FOR THE WORLD

Words and Music by KYE FLEMING,
DENNIS MORGAN and CHARLES QUILLEN

Lyrics:

Our paths may nev-er cross a-gain.
They say that all good things must end.

May-be my heart will nev-er mend,
Love comes and goes just like the wind.

but I'm glad for all the good times. You brought me so
You've got your dreams to fol-low, but if I had the

I LOVE

Words and Music by
TOM T. HALL

(I Never Promised You A)
ROSE GARDEN

Words and Music by
JOE SOUTH

I WALK THE LINE

Words and Music by
JOHN R. CASH

1. I keep a close watch on this heart of
2. ver - y eas - y to be
3.-5. *(See additional lyrics)*

mine._____ I keep my eyes wide
true._____ I find my - self a - lone

o - pen all the time._____ I keep the
when each day is through._____ Yes, I'll ad -

Additional Lyrics

3. As sure as night is dark and day is light,
I keep you on my mind both day and night.
And happiness I've known proves that it's right.
Because you're mine I walk the line.

4. You've got a way to keep me on your side.
You give me cause for love that I can't hide.
For you I know I'd even try to turn the tide.
Because you're mine I walk the line.

5. I keep a close watch on this heart of mine.
I keep my eyes wide open all the time.
I keep the ends out for the tie that binds.
Because you're mine I walk the line.

I WAS COUNTRY WHEN COUNTRY WASN'T COOL

Words and Music by KYE FLEMING
and DENNIS MORGAN

I ____ was coun-try from my hat down to my ____ boots. I still act ____ and look the same; ____ what you see ain't noth-in' new. ____ I was coun-try, ____ when coun-try was-n't cool. ____

Additional Lyrics

2. I remember circling the drive-in,
   Pulling up, and turning down George Jones.
   I remember when no one was looking,
   I was putting peanuts in my coke.
   I took a lot of kidding, 'cause I never did fit in;
   Now look at everybody trying to be what I was then;
   I was country, when country wasn't cool.

3. They called us country bumpkins for sticking to our roots;
   I'm just glad we're in a country where we're all free to choose;
   I was country, when country wasn't cool.

I'M SO LONESOME I COULD CRY

Words and Music by
HANK WILLIAMS

Hear ____ that lone - some whip - poor - will, he sounds ____ too
ev - er see ____ a rob - in weep when leaves ____ be-

blue ____ to fly. ____ The mid - night train is
gan ____ to die. ____ That mid - means night he's lost is the

whin - ing low. I'm so lone - some I could _ cry. ____
will to live. I'm so lone - some I could _ cry. ____

I'M SORRY

Words and Music by RONNIE SELF
and DUB ALBRITTEN

IN THE MISTY MOONLIGHT

Words and Music by
CINDY WALKER

I.O.U.

Words and Music by KERRY CHATER
and AUSTIN ROBERTS

Moderately slow Ballad

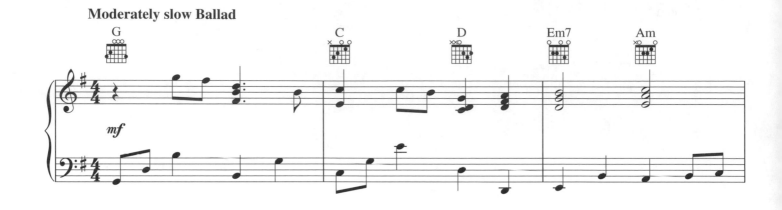

You be-lieve that I've changed your life for-ev-er and you're
mazed when you say it's me you live for and you

nev-er gon-na find an-oth-er some-bod-y like me. And you
know that when I'm hold-ing you, you're right where you be-long. And, my

G D7 C Am7 D
U. more than life, now more than ev - er. I
G G/F# Em To Coda Am7 D7sus 1 G
know that it's the sweet-est debt I'll ev - er have to pay.
C D7sus D11 5fr 2 G D7sus D.S. al Coda
I'm a - And I. O.
CODA Am7 D7sus G C D G
ev - er have to pay.
rit.
a tempo
rit.

IT WAS ALMOST LIKE A SONG

Lyric by HAL DAVID
Music by ARCHIE JORDAN

Once in ev-'ry life, some-one comes a -
You were in my arms, just where you be -

long, and you came to me.)
long, we were so in love.)

IT'S HARD TO BE HUMBLE

Words and Music by
MAC DAVIS

Oh, Lord, it's hard _____ to be hum - ble

when you're per - fect in ev - er - y way. _____

I can't wait to look in _____ the mir - ror

JEALOUS HEART

Words and Music by
JENNY LOU CARSON

IT'S ONLY MAKE BELIEVE

Words and Music by CONWAY TWITTY
and JACK NANCE

Peo-ple see us ev-'ry-where, they think you real-ly care, but my-self I can't de-ceive, I know it's on-ly make be-lieve. My one and on-ly prayer is that some-day you'll care,

THE LAST WORD IN LONESOME IS ME

Words and Music by
ROGER MILLER

To Coda

lone - ly, the last word in lone - some is me. _____

_____ Too bad what's hap - pened _____ to our good

love, _____ too bad what's hap - pened _____ to our good

love. Some - times our best is - n't quite good e -

LITTLE GREEN APPLES

Words and Music by
BOBBY RUSSELL

THE LONG BLACK VEIL

Words and Music by MARIJOHN WILKIN
and DANNY DILL

Ten years a- go ____ on a cold, dark
judge said, "Son, what is your al - i -

night ____ some - one was killed 'neath the
bi? If you were some - where killed else, then you

town hall light. There were few at the
won't have to die." I ____ spoke not a

LUCILLE

Words and Music by ROGER BOWLING
and HAL BYNUM

In a bar in To-
mir - ror, I
Af - ter he

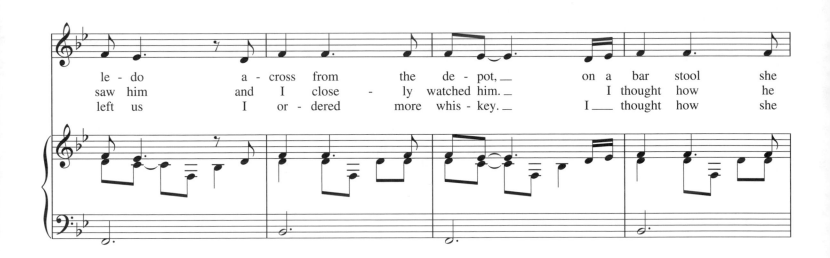

le - do a - cross from the de - pot,___ on a bar stool she
saw him and I close - ly watched him.___ I thought how he
left us I or - dered more whis - key.___ I___ thought how she

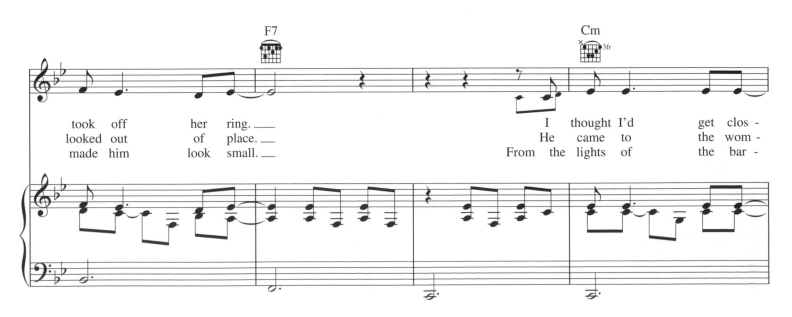

took off her ring.___ I thought I'd get clos-
looked out of place.___ He came to the wom-
made him look small.___ From the lights of the bar-

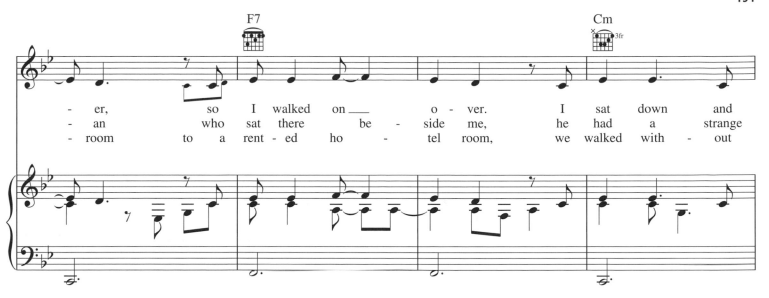

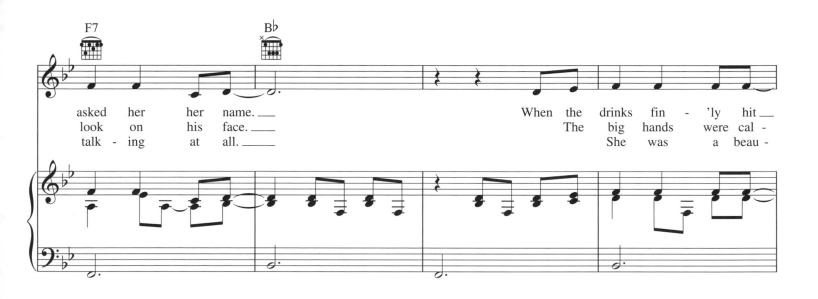

liv - ing on dreams. I'm hun - gry for
thought I was dead. But he start - ed
I'd lost my mind. I could - n't

laugh - ter and here ev - er af - ter I'm af - ter what - ev -
shak - ing, his big heart was break - ing, he
hold her, 'cause the words that he told her kept

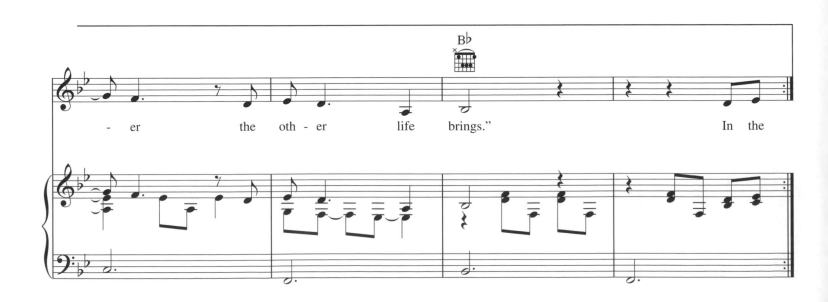

- er the oth - er life brings." In the

turned to the wom-an and said:)
com - ing back time af - ter time.)

You picked a

fine time to leave ___ me, Lu - cille,

with

four hun - gry chil - dren and a crop in the field.

I've had some bad times, _ lived through some

MOUNTAIN OF LOVE

Words and Music by
HAROLD DORMAN

LUCKENBACH, TEXAS
(Back to the Basics of Love)

Words and Music by BOBBY EMMONS
and CHIPS MOMAN

The on-ly two things in life that make it worth liv-in' is

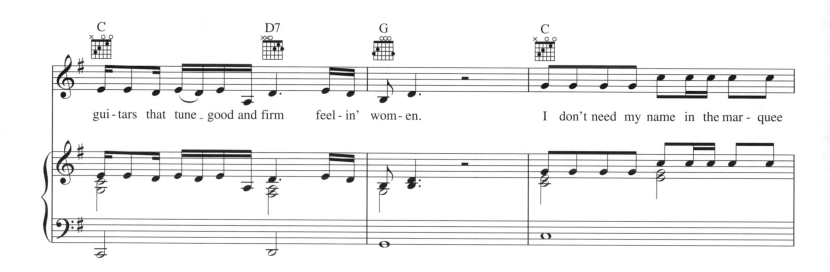

gui-tars that tune good and firm feel-in' wom-en. I don't need my name in the mar-quee

lights; I got my song and I got you with me to-night. May-be it's time we got

MY HEROES HAVE ALWAYS BEEN COWBOYS

Words and Music by
SHARON VAUGHN

MY SON CALLS ANOTHER MAN DADDY

Words and Music by HANK WILLIAMS
and JEWELL HOUSE

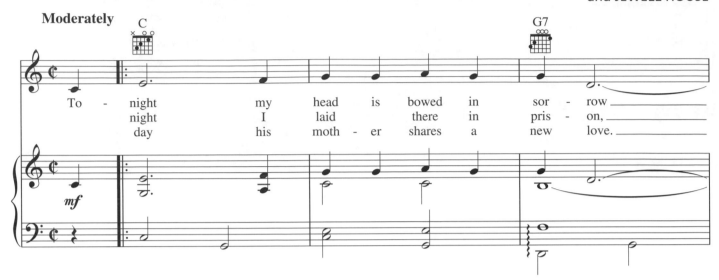

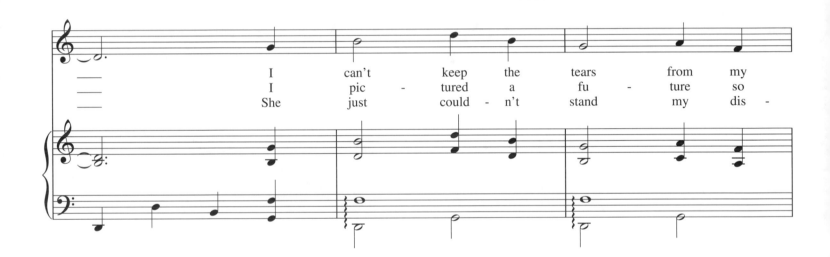

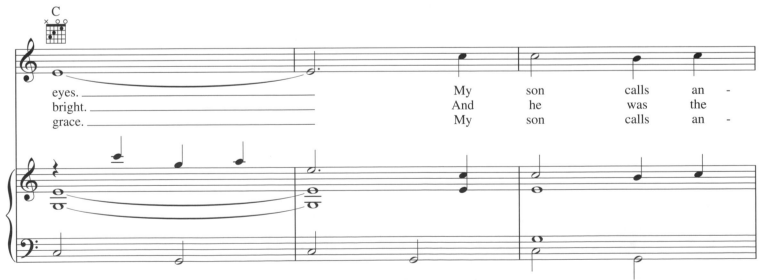

name or my face.

God on - ly knows how it hurts me,

for an - oth - er to be in my

1, 2

place.

{ Each
{ To -

3

place.

8vb⌡

OH, LONESOME ME

Words and Music by
DON GIBSON

NOBODY LIKES SAD SONGS

By WAYLAND HOLYFIELD
and BOB McDILL

You've seen the way I en-ter-tain a crowd;

I used to pack 'em in _____ from miles a-round. _____

And I'd play the hap-py songs that made 'em smile. _____

Lyrics:

since you went _ a - way, _____ seems like sad ____ songs _ are

all I can play. _____

The crowd gets rest - less and they drift a - way.
The boss just told me things aren't go - ing well.

OKIE FROM MUSKOGEE

Words and Music by MERLE HAGGARD
and ROY EDWARD BURRIS

We don't smoke mar-i-jua-na in Mus-ko-gee, _____ and
We don't make a par-ty out of lov-ing, _____ but
boots are still in style if a man needs foot-wear, _____ but

we don't take our trips on L.S. D. and we don't burn our
we like hold-ing hands and pitch-ing woo. We don't let our
beads and Ro-man san-dals won't be seen. Foot-ball's still the

draft cards down on Main Street, but we like liv-ing
hair grow long and shag-gy like the hip-pies out in
rough-est thing on cam-pus, and the kids here still re-

ON THE ROAD AGAIN

Words and Music by
WILLIE NELSON

Lively Two-Beat

On the

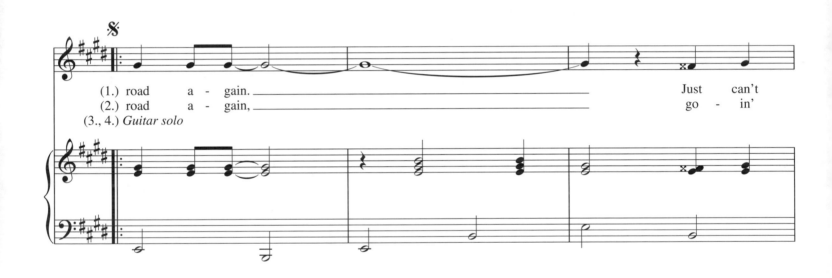

(1.) road a - gain. _____
(2.) road a - gain, _____
(3., 4.) *Guitar solo*

Just can't
go - in'

wait to get on the road a - gain. _____ The life I
plac - es that I've nev - er been, _____ see - in'

A RAINY NIGHT IN GEORGIA

Words and Music by
TONY JOE WHITE

1. Hov-erin' by my suit-case, tryin' to find a warm place to
2. Ne-on signs a-flash-in', tax-i-cabs and bus-es pass-in'
3. (See additional lyrics)

spend the night; a heav-y rain a-fall-in';
through the night; the dis-tant moan-in' of a train

seems I hear your voice call-in', "It's all right."
seems to play a sad re-frain to the night:

Chorus

A rain-y night in Geor-gia, a rain-y night in Geor-gia; _____ I be-lieve it's rain-in' all _____ o-ver the world.

How man-y times I've won-dered,

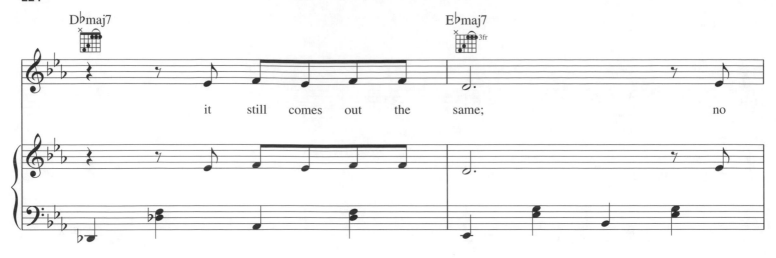

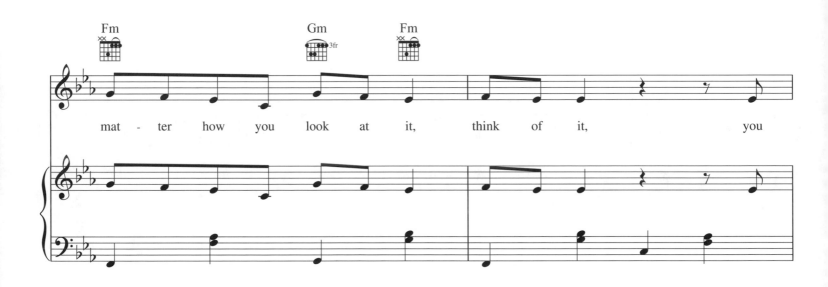

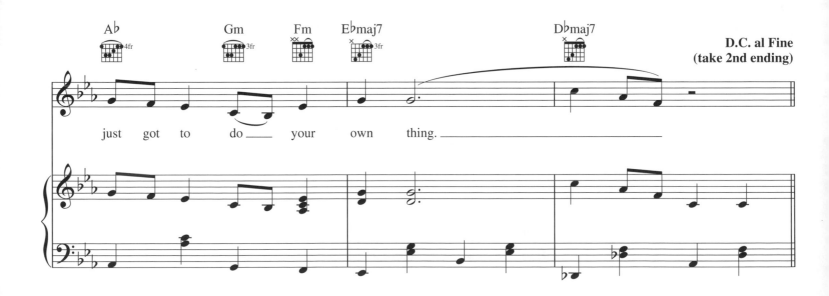

Additional Lyrics

3. I find me a place in a box car,
   So I take out my guitar to pass some time;
   Late at night when it's hard to rest,
   I hold your picture to my chest, and I'm all right.
   Chorus

SHARE YOUR LOVE WITH ME

Words and Music by DEADRIC MALONE
and AL BRAGGS

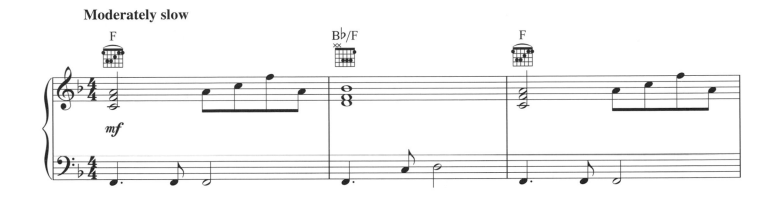

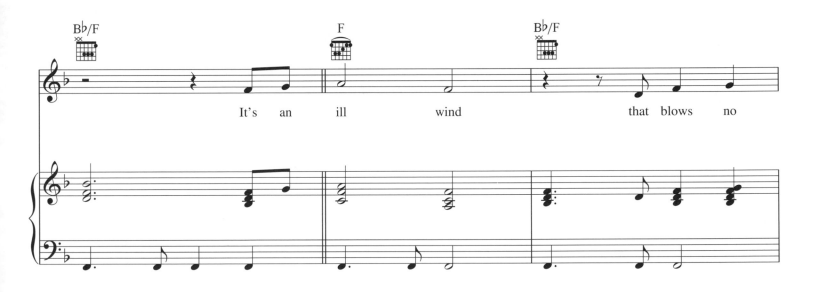

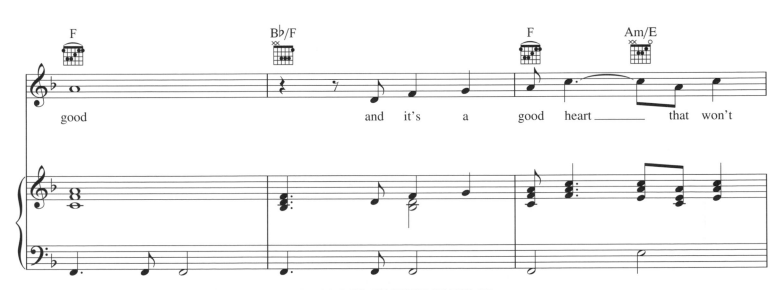

RUBY, DON'T TAKE YOUR LOVE TO TOWN

Words and Music by
MEL TILLIS

SINGING THE BLUES

Words and Music by
MELVIN ENDSLEY

SMOKY MOUNTAIN RAIN

Words and Music by KYE FLEMING
and DENNIS MORGAN

I thumbed my way from L.
I waved a die - sel down

A. back to Knox - ville.
out - side a ca - fe.
I found
He said that

out those bright lights ain't where _ I be - long. _____
he was going as far as _____ Gat - lin - burg. _____

SON-OF-A-PREACHER MAN

Words and Music by JOHN HURLEY
and RONNIE WILKINS

Jim- my Ray was a preach - er's son. When his dad - dy would vis- it, he'd come___ a - long.
When they gath- ered 'round the par- lor talk- in', cous- in Jim- my would take me walk- in'. Out through the back yard

Be- in' good is - n't al - ways eas- y ___ no mat- ter how ___ I try. When he start - ed sweet talk- in' to me,
he'd come 'n tell me ev- 'ry- thing is al - right, kiss and tell me ev- 'ry-

SWINGIN'

Words and Music by JOHN DAVID ANDERSON
and LIONEL DELMORE

1. There's _____ a lit-tle girl in our neigh-bor-hood, her
2.,3. *(See additional lyrics)*

name is Char-lotte John-son, and she's real-ly look-ing good. I had to go and see her, so I

called her on the phone. I walked o-ver to her house, _ and this was go-in' on: 2. Her

Char-lotte, she's as pret-ty as the an-gels when they sing.___ I can't be-lieve I'm out here on her

front porch in the swing, just a-swing-in.'___ (Swing-in,___

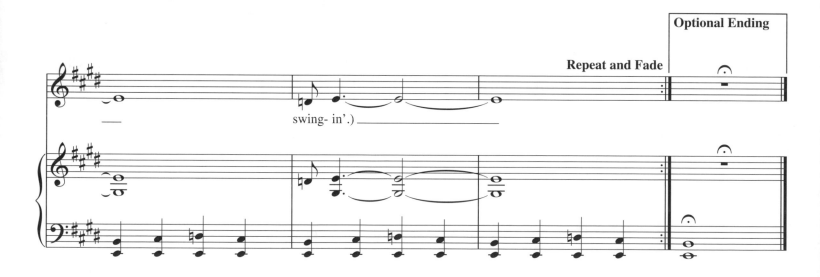

Optional Ending

Repeat and Fade

___ swing-in'.) ___

Additional Lyrics

2. Her brother was on the sofa
Eatin' chocolate pie.
Her mama was in the kitchen
Cuttin' chicken up to fry.
Her daddy was in the backyard
Rollin' up a garden hose.
I was on the porch with Charlotte
Feelin' love down to my toes,
Chorus

3. Now Charlotte, she's a darlin';
She's the apple of my eye.
When I'm on the swing with her
It makes me almost high.
And Charlotte is my lover.
And she has been since the spring.
I just can't believe it started
On her front porch in the swing.
Chorus

WATERLOO

Words and Music by JOHN LOUDERMILK
and MARIJOHN WILKINS

WHEN YOU'RE HOT, YOU'RE HOT

Words and Music by
JERRY REED HUBBARD

(Spoken:) Well now,

me and Homer Jones and Big John Talley had a   big crap game goin' back in the alley; and
time I rolled 'em   dice I'd win, and I would   just get ready to roll 'em again, when I
took us into court I couldn't believe my eyes.   The judge was a fishin' buddy that I recognized. I said, "Hey

I kept rollin' them   sevens   and winnin' all   them pots.   My
heard something behind me and I turned around and there was a big ole cop.   He said,
judge, old buddy, old pal,   I'll pay you that hundred I owe you if you get me out of this spot." So he

254

A WHITE SPORT COAT
(And a Pink Carnation)

Words and Music by
MARTY ROBBINS

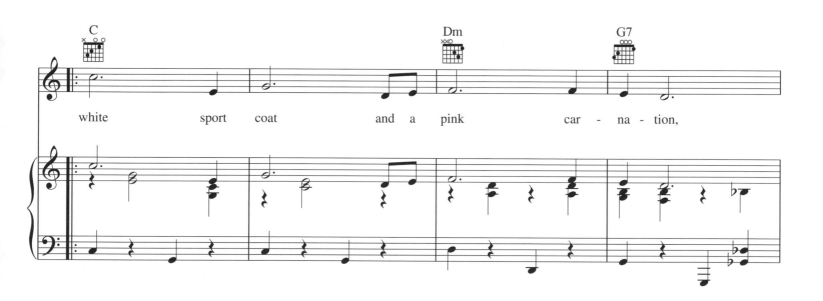

white sport coat and a pink car - na - tion,

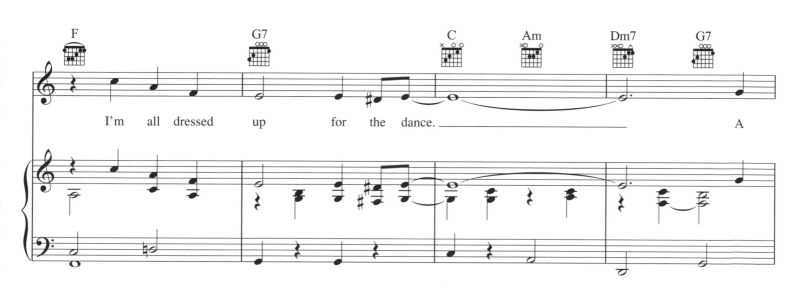

I'm all dressed up for the dance. _____ A

YOU DECORATED MY LIFE

Words and Music by DEBBIE HUPP
and BOB MORRISON

by paint-ing your love _____ all o-ver my heart. __

You dec-o-rat-ed my __ life. _____

Like a

YOU WIN AGAIN

Words and Music by
HANK WILLIAMS

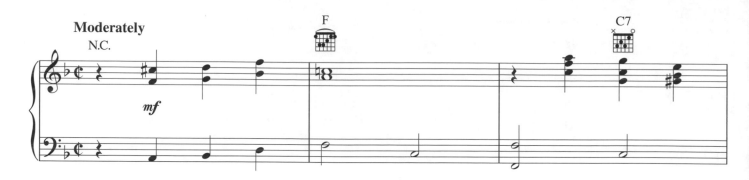

The news is out ___ all o - ver
for ___ your vic - tim

town ___ that you've been seen ___ a - run - nin'
now ___ 'cause soon his head ___ like mine will

bod - y knew but me.
love and give the blame.

Just trust - ing you was my great
I guess that I should not com -

sin. What can I do, you win a -
plain, I love you still, you win a -

gain. I'm sor - ry gain.

rit.

YOU'RE THE REASON GOD MADE OKLAHOMA

Words and Music by SANDY PINKARD,
LARRY COLLINS, BOUDLEAUX BRYANT
and FELICE BRYANT

Medium Country Blues

1. There's a full _____ moon o - ver Tul - sa. I hope that it's shin - in' on you. _____
2. (See additional lyrics)

_____ The nights are get - tin' cold - er in Cher - o - kee coun - try, there's a

Blue Nor - ther pass - in' through. _____ I re - mem - ber green eyes _ and a ranch - er's daugh - ter, but re-

Additional Lyrics

2. Here the city lights outshine the moon,
I was just now thinking of you.
Sometimes when the wind blows you can see the mountains
And all the way to Malibu.
Everyone's a star here in L.A. country,
You ought to see the things that they do.
All the cowboys down on the Sunset Strip
Wish they could be like you.
The Santa Monica Freeway
Sometimes makes a country girl blue.
Chorus

3. I worked ten hours on a John Deere tractor,
Just thinkin of you all day...
I've got a calico cat and a two room flat.
On a street in West L.A.
Chorus

YOUR CHEATIN' HEART

Words and Music by
HANK WILLIAMS

Moderately

Your cheat - in' ___ heart ___ will make you weep. ___
heart ___ will pine some - day ___

You'll cry and ___ cry ___ and try to
and crave the ___ love ___ you threw a -

sleep. ___ But sleep won't ___ come ___
way. ___ The time will ___ come ___